Life
Is
Good

Books by Amy Hall

*Getting Your Groove Back: The Sassy
Woman's Guide to Recharging Your Life*

The Joy of Being a Woman

Postcards from the '80s: 80 Lists to Remember

Life Is Good

888 Reasons Why

AMY HALL

**Andrews McMeel
Publishing**

Kansas City

02 03 04 05 06 BIN 10 9 8 7 6 5 4 3 2 1

ISBN: 0-7407-1888-6

Library of Congress Control Card
Number: 2001086769

Book design by Lisa Martin

ATTENTION: SCHOOLS AND BUSINESSES

A *Special thanks* to these beloved
contributors who so kindly shared both their
serious and sassy opinions on the wonderful,
everyday gifts that life provides us . . .

Steve Davis
Jennifer Flok
Leslie Faulkner Gage
Lisa Garrison
Dora Mainwaring Golding
Joe Golding
Lauren Katz
Scott Keepers
Martin LeRoy
Jennifer Mills
Ken Milman
Leigh Powell
Emöke Pulay
Bryan Shelby
Erik Slangerup
Brett Weiss
Scott Wells
Jim Wilkerson
Laura Wilkerson
Stephanie Williamson

For my strong and loving Sophia,
my larger-than-life Zack & Logan,
& my determined and tough Molly & Mira,
Heed the call to the fun
and zany adventure that your lives will be.

For Joe and Dora and pots of tea

For Scott and a million wonderful moments

Introduction

Life *is* good.

It's true—life is wonderful. Every day, there are tons of tranquil, fantastic moments and doses of magic. However, this simple declaration is certain to meet with some initial controversy in your skeptical mind. Why? Because as a culture we've nearly wholeheartedly accepted the notion of life as a day-to-day struggle designed to overpower us, as a fairly weary and thankless enterprise. I think that's wrong. The problem is not with our lives; it's with us. Our perspective has become so jaded in this material world that we have blinded ourselves to the multitude of daily habits, rituals, and events that cumulatively provide us with great pleasure and delight. What more can be said? Certainly heartache and tragedy visit us occasionally, but going on in the background of all daily life are the little things that can truly inject us with comfort and bliss. Every enjoyment to be had around us, no matter how small it may appear, is a miracle in time and space—and should be viewed as nothing short of spectacular. Read on to celebrate and recognize 888 of the *many* reasons why life is wonderful, good, and magnificent!

Life Is Good

· 1 ·

Adrenaline rushes from riding
incredible roller coasters and
relishing the pit in your stomach
you get from plummeting down two
hundred feet of a hissing steel track

· 2 ·

The sheer luxury of a hot
and sudsy shower after getting
home from a camping trip

· 3 ·

No line at the grocery store
when your cart is full

• 4 •

The occasional drink of
a glass of cold whole milk

• 5 •

Getting a long e-mail or letter
from a friend with whom you've
been out of touch (Although I have
to say of the two, it's a particular
treat to finger a real manila envelope
in your hand as you stroll back to
the front door these days.)

Life Is Good

• 6 •

Aimless Sunday drives on forgotten
back roads where you may actually
drive on gravel as you spy the
cows and barbwire fences

• 7 •

The smell of a *homemade*
pumpkin pie coming from the
kitchen at Thanksgiving

· 8 ·

Hearing a favorite song on the
radio while trapped in traffic and
turning the volume up

· 9 ·

Lying quietly in bed and
listening to the spring rains roll
in against the window

· 10 ·

A boisterous game of cards
with friends full of playful haggling
about rules and table talk

Life Is Good

· 11 ·

Serious games of footsie

· 12 ·

Finding that the warm cashmere
sweater you want is on sale for half
price after you've already fallen in love
with it in the dressing-room mirror

· 13 ·

Thick chocolate milkshakes poured
out of those stainless-steel shake tins
into your tall glass (The "bendy" straws
they usually come with are nice, too.)

· 14 ·

Having a stash of slick
grape Popsicles to nurse
when it's hot outside

· 15 ·

Watching a litter of kittens
attack one another's tails,
or a passerby's shoestrings

· 16 ·

Licking the chocolate icing
off yellow cupcakes

· 17 ·

The clacking sound
of plastic checkers being moved
around a checkerboard

· 18 ·

Those mornings when you
check the alarm clock and
realize you still have a few
hours left to sleep

Life Is Good

· 19 ·

Free samples at the grocery store or
mall food court—there's just something
great about getting munchies for free

· 20 ·

Licking the dough off your fingers
after you've slid the pan of chocolate
chip cookies inside the oven

· 21 ·

The rhythmic zipping sounds
of a fly fisherman at work
with his rod and reel

• 22 •

Swinging on swings like you
did as a kid—leaning way back
in your seat when your feet
are turned toward the sky

• 23 •

The dawn of a brand new day.
I think the act of waking up and
regaining awareness is a bit mystical.

• 24 •

Using a small spoon so you can
savor each little slurp of warm soup

· 25 ·

The near-ethereal scent
of a freshly mowed lawn

· 26 ·

Warm clothes and towels
right out of the dryer

· 27 ·

The electric hiss of a
snowboard gliding quickly
and smoothly over snow

· 28 ·

Most any barefoot
moment spent at a beach

· 29 ·

Tattered boxer shorts
still so comfortable they
cannot yet be retired

· 30 ·

Catching a moment of a soap opera
in Spanish and trying to figure out
what melodrama has unfolded

Life Is Good

· 31 ·

New-car smell

· 32 ·

The humor of how the Y2K bug
didn't end the world as we know it

· 33 ·

The grace of the perfect
rock-skip across a pond

· 34 ·

Overhearing someone speaking
complimentarily of you

Life Is Good

· 35 ·

A ski trip moment: spending
midnight on top of a snow-covered
mountain, looking at the stars
above and town lights below

· 36 ·

The bench in front of
your favorite piece of work
at the local art museum

· 37 ·

The time of peaceful reflection
that comes from soaking in a quiet
bubble bath and candlelight

Life Is Good

• 38 •

The song of the ice-cream
man's truck in summertime

• 39 •

"Make-up" sex

• 40 •

Watching the snowflakes
of winter coat the yard
in a slow progression

· 41 ·

The rising sun's red and orange
explosion onto the sky

· 42 ·

That one restaurant
that offers sweetened tea in
a glass brimming with ice

· 43 ·

All the humorous things the
neighbors seem to do from your
vantage point on the back porch

• 44 •

The thrilling anticipation in the
maternity ward waiting room

• 45 •

Long Sunday afternoon
naps on the couch

• 46 •

The raw exertion and burning
in your thigh muscles from
hiking up a steep slope

Life Is Good

· 47 ·

The snapping sound
as you pull a ripe apple
or pear off its tree

· 48 ·

The ticklish feel of dewy
grass between your feet

· 49 ·

Taking in the fall of evening in
a rocking chair you keep in motion
with delicate lifts of your heels

• 50 •

The men in movies who
always forget to grab *the* suitcase
before they rush their pregnant
wives to the hospital

• 51 •

Fireworks. No explanation of
pyrotechnic mechanics ever makes
them seem less magical when they
 boom into the sky
    and explode
     in color as a
    chorus of arms
    points upward.

· 52 ·

The crisp sound of ice skates
coming to a swift stop at the rink

· 53 ·

Holding hands in the special
manner that feels "right" to you

· 54 ·

Playing catch with a dog on a beach
and watching her dive fearlessly
into the surf ("Geneva" of Santa
Barbara is one golden retriever
I'll personally challenge any day
with a half-chewed tennis ball.)

· 55 ·

Deliberating what
cloud shapes look like

· 56 ·

Catching the largest fish
you've ever caught and then
releasing it back into the green
depths with a splash

· 57 ·

Silently holding the person
you love in your arms

· 58 ·

Flapping your plastic
flippers around as you snorkel
along an ocean reef

· 59 ·

Sheets with a high thread count

· 60 ·

The off-beat rhythms
of the plethora of tap shoes
during the kiddie dance recital

· 61 ·

Coloring at any age—smearing
waxy crayon color onto a page
is a piece of heaven

· 62 ·

Reading *The Cat in the Hat*

· 63 ·

Your lips pressed against the rim
of a delicate white china teacup

· 64 ·

Only a very small percentage of
the things that could go wrong
with a body actually go wrong.
We have a lot of moving parts,
so be thankful for the myriad of
parts that keep on ticking just
fine—like your faithful big toe.

· 65 ·

Wriggling out sand from
between your toes as you finish
a stroll along the shore

• 66 •

The soothing cadence
of the voices on NPR

• 67 •

Your favorite cheap wine that's
so inexpensive you can always
treat yourself to a shiny bottle

• 68 •

Creeks and rivers that
still have lots of turtles sunning
on rocks and frogs splashing
and croaking away

· 69 ·

Dogs with pitiful big brown eyes
rolling over for belly rubs

· 70 ·

The rippling of
plush red curtains
being opened and closed

· 71 ·

The soft sound of the razor
smoothly shaving your skin

• 72 •

Wild dolphins joining you as
you swim in the ocean (After you
realize they aren't of the *Jaws*
persuasion it's very
enjoyable.)

• 73 •

The soothing swing
of a large hammock hung
between two oak trees

Life Is Good

· 74 ·

A caring friend or relative
who will sleep beside your bed
during a hospital stay

· 75 ·

Afternoons spent strolling on
crunchy fall leaves and rubbing
your mitten-clad hands together

· 76 ·

The sense of euphoric
accomplishment that caps
off a day spent gardening and
landscaping in your yard

· 77 ·

The clacking of plastic
poker chips being stacked
on one another

· 78 ·

The nostalgic feel of a well-worn
leather baseball mitt

· 79 ·

Cotton-candy stickiness
coating your fingers
at the carnival

· 80 ·

The pleasant part of a road
trip where you realize you're
in the middle of nowhere
and not caring, merely
listening to the radio and
watching the scenery pass by

· 81 ·

Simple but luxuriously
fulfilling dinners composed of
Brie, grapes, wine, and bread

· 82 ·

Bubble wrap exploding
in a chorus of pops under
the meticulous massaging
of your hands (forget about
$100 per hour therapy)

· 83 ·

The overwhelming and
unconditional bond you feel
with your child the first moment
you see her live and in the
cradle of your arms

Life Is Good

• 84 •

Deep-tissue neck massages
from experienced hands

• 85 •

The comfort of slipping out
of contacts at the end of the day
and putting on your glasses

• 86 •

The perfect apple crisp:
gooey apple chunks evenly covered
with crunchy, buttery granules
that melt on your tongue

Life Is Good

· 87 ·

The chicken dance and
its funky signature music

· 88 ·

The sound of checkers falling down
the slots of a Connect Four game

· 89 ·

Munching on hot authentic
bratwurst in Germany when
you're starved from walking
around museums

· 90 ·

The window seat on a long
flight where you can daydream
while watching the clouds roll
by in white serenity

· 91 ·

Sliding ice chips around in your
mouth with your tongue

· 92 ·

New white socks on your feet,
anytime, anywhere

• 93 •

The gleeful squeak of
markers on a whiteboard

• 94 •

Sunrise—the color
scheme just can't be beat.

• 95 •

Kneading biscuit dough
with your hands and feeling
the flour coat your skin

· 96 ·

There's still as much pleasure in
riding a bike with no hands as there
was when you were ten.

· 97 ·

The nightly ritual of curling
up in bed with a wonderful
book at your fingertips

· 98 ·

The shimmer of a green
dragonfly's delicate wings hovering
at the edge of a puddle

Life Is Good

• 99 •

The ritual of sprawling out on the
floor with the rustling Sunday paper
and nursing a cup of gourmet coffee
while still in your pajamas

• 100 •

The exquisite softness of the fur
under your cat's chin

Life Is Good

• 101 •

The rhythmic snipping
of hedge trimmers cleaning
up a row of shrubs

• 102 •

The rich smells of roasted
beans and the swishing
sounds of espresso machines
in a bustling coffee shop

• 103 •

The ethereal quality
of *any* piece of bagpipe music

Life Is Good

· 104 ·

The first footprints
on a virgin snow

· 105 ·

The sensation of
giving your "all"

· 106 ·

Getting all "ver klimpt"
by the cuteness of every
ensemble you see while
shopping for baby clothes

· 107 ·

A crisp, buttery grilled cheese
and a bowl of chicken noodle
soup on a winter afternoon

· 108 ·

The wonderful surprise
of receiving a funny
card from a friend

· 109 ·

Smothering your lips with soothing
cherry-scented Chapstick

Life Is Good

· 110 ·

The unadulterated smell of
a just-opened box of crayons

· 111 ·

The way your sunburned skin
gratefully drinks up aloe vera

· 112 ·

The snap of placing the
cap of a pen back on

· 113 ·

The hypnotizing movements of
sea life inside a grand-scale
aquarium (The jellyfish of
Monterey Bay Aquarium
deserve a good twenty
minutes of observation.)

· 114 ·

Watching orange powder
dissolve in a whirlpool as
you mix up a glass of Tang

Life Is Good

· 115 ·

Closing your eyes
and listening to
Ray Charles sing "Georgia"

· 116 ·

Sleeping naked in the
hot summer months

· 117 ·

The ticklish brushwork a
Mendi hand tattoo requires

· 118 ·

Voyaging to a museum or city to
see the one famous thing you've
always loved and wanted to see
in person so you can declare
with joy that "It is real!
It exists! I have seen it!"

· 119 ·

The artful hand-massaging of an
excellent manicurist who has
coated your palms with lotion

· 120 ·

Slathering gobs of icing on a
German chocolate cake with
a spatula you occasionally lick

· 121 ·

The familiar creaking
boards of a worn footbridge

· 122 ·

Carving pumpkins in October so you
can scoop out the sweet-smelling
flesh and get up-to-your-elbows in
fun goop before you toast the seeds

· 123 ·

The delicate arc of a white
orchid leaning in its bowl

· 124 ·

Almond slivers on
casseroles and pastries

Life Is Good

• 125 •

Admiring your shiny shoes
as you leave the shoeshine
stand in the airport

• 126 •

Dragging a feather or straw
along the carpet in front of a cat
and watching its ears go back
and neck hairs rise

• 127 •

The cushy armchairs at
your local Barnes & Noble

Life Is Good

· 128 ·

The feel of new underwear against
your skin (It's your little secret the
day you break it in, too.)

· 129 ·

Fruitcake jokes
at Christmas time

· 130 ·

The moment when candlelight
expires as you lightly blow it out

· 131 ·

The smell of a row of grapes
in a vineyard—the sweet, earthy
aroma of a wine soon to be

· 132 ·

The subtle sound of peeling
a sticky note up from its pad

· 133 ·

The peace of floating in a canoe,
stopping in the midst of a journey
downstream and just taking
in your surroundings

Life Is Good

· 134 ·

Your grateful feet after
you kick off your shoes

· 135 ·

Reliving your childhood
through the musty and tattered
pages of your old comic books

· 136 ·

A beautiful soprano
voice singing in a
New York City theater

· 137 ·

The rush of becoming airborne
when launching off a dock
to parasail—you are finally
floating upward like a bird

· 138 ·

The wonderful splashing
of children's rubber rain boots
stomping in puddles

· 139 ·

The cool, dimply feel
of a golf ball in hand

· 140 ·

Sucking meat off of Memphis'
Rendezvous ribs while your
fingertips are covered with
sauce and seasonings

· 141 ·

The sneaky feeling you get in
the pit of your stomach while
reading off-color material or
hearing dirty jokes

Life Is Good

· 142 ·

The surreal quality of making
love in the middle of the night

· 143 ·

The cadence of the prayer
spoken by a family on the
first night of Hanukkah

· 144 ·

Birth announcements from friends
featuring funny pictures of the proud
parents' predictably alien-like baby

• 145 •

The sound of peeling
the plastic wrap off a new CD

• 146 •

Spirited performances
of "Dueling Banjos"

Life Is Good

· 147 ·

The ritual of leisurely bobbing a tea
bag up and down in your teacup

· 148 ·

The crisp feel of a clean shirt with
just the right amount of starch

· 149 ·

The sweet echoes caused by a
basketball dribbled in the driveway

Life Is Good

· 150 ·

Waking up cold in the middle
of the night and slinking over to
your mate's side of the bed for
the best warmth you can get

· 151 ·

The fantastic smell that filters
through your car every time you
drive past a bread bakery

· 152 ·

Those late showers
on weekend afternoons

Life Is Good

· 153 ·

Feeding the shiny Koi fish that
come right to your hand for
bread bits in Oriental gardens

· 154 ·

The accidental facial you get
when you take the lid off a pot
of water boiling on the stove

· 155 ·

The pop from opening
a new can of tennis balls

· 156 ·

Thunder rumblings in the distance,
signaling an oncoming storm

· 157 ·

Chewing Gummi bears

· 158 ·

Nights spent sleeping in a pup tent
pitched by the kids in the backyard

Life Is Good

· 159 ·

Being able to rely on
someone to fill your emergency
prescription at 2 A.M.

· 160 ·

The "off" button on your cell phone

· 161 ·

The near-operatic chorus
of the million crickets outside
a country home at night

· 162 ·

Sprawling out on the cold earth to
make the perfect snow angel

· 163 ·

The smooth feel of
the ball of your ankle

· 164 ·

Books by Judy Blume

Life Is Good

· 165 ·

The sound caused by rubbing
slick snowsuits and raincoats

· 166 ·

The way your feet sink ankle-deep
into the moistened sand at the
edge of a beach as waves lap in

· 167 ·

The smell emanating from the
Cinnabon station at the mall

Life Is Good

· 168 ·

All the free public restrooms
available for your use when
you really have to go

· 169 ·

Discovering an artifact or painting
you've always loved in the new
museum you are just now exploring

· 170 ·

Seeing that shiny, small
hummingbirds have finally
discovered your new feeder

· 171 ·

Steaming Jacuzzis with jets
that pummel your calf muscles
when you're completely
sore from exercising

· 172 ·

The sound of Legos
clicking together

· 173 ·

The way the open box of Tide
washing detergent freshens the
scent of the entire laundry room

Life Is Good

· 174 ·

Sliding around on a slick Twister
board after flipping the spinner

· 175 ·

The perfect cotton-soft
inside of a new sweatshirt

· 176 ·

The pop of opening a fresh
new bag of Lay's potato chips

· 177 ·

The quiet solitude and sense of
delicious sneakiness from being
the first one up in the morning
and shaking around the cereal
box in the kitchen

· 178 ·

Gallivanting across wine country
and finding a restaurant with a
table overlooking the vineyards
where you can smoke cigars
after enjoying the company
of good friends, good food,
and, of course, good wine

Life Is Good

· 179 ·

The clicking of castanets

· 180 ·

The hypnotic effect
of a flickering candle flame

· 181 ·

The smell in the air
before a snowfall

Life Is Good

· 182 ·

Walking through the Botanical
Gardens of Berlin in the fall
with a good sweater on

· 183 ·

The faint spritzing sounds
of a bottle of perfume in use

· 184 ·

Tambourines (My all-time high music-
wise was when a band let me take
the stage with them and play this
wonderful instrument—long story!)

Life Is Good

· 185 ·

The faint crunching sound from
sinking into a feather bed that
molds around your body

· 186 ·

The taste of a really sweet cigar

· 187 ·

The vibrant red flesh
of a tomato fresh
from the garden

· 188 ·

The rush from spying a famous
politician, athlete, actress,
or author out in public

· 189 ·

Eating raw cookie dough out of
the fridge at 2 A.M. and washing
it down with chocolate milk
(the epitome of decadence in
which anyone can indulge)

· 190 ·

The pleasant hissing sound
and puffs of steam emitted by
a faithful iron at work

· 191 ·

Picking dandelions and popping
off the heads with your thumbnail—
sure it's an odd form of release,
but somehow no one can
resist the exercise

Life Is Good

· 192 ·

That delicious moment
of anticipation as you pull
out of your driveway for a
long-awaited road trip

· 193 ·

Slowly dripping honey onto
anything (be it foodstuffs or
a person)—it's just a good,
natural feeling

· 194 ·

Lifting up the lid to check on the
warm pot of chamomile
tea still steeping on
the kitchen
counter

· 195 ·

Marvelously colorful stacks of
in-season fruits and veggies at
the produce stand on an otherwise
bland city street—it's as if you are
witnessing a direct proclamation
from Mother Nature herself

Life Is Good

· 196 ·

Cats swatting at your feet
in the wee hours as you move
them around under the covers

· 197 ·

The clicking and snapping
of a Rubik's Cube in hand

· 198 ·

Sleeping on freshly laundered sheets
after you yourself took a late-night
shower or bath—it's the epitome
of feeling clean and fresh

Life Is Good

· 199 ·

Treetops covered with
fresh snow, first thing in the
morning when you wake

· 200 ·

Licking sprinkles off sugar cookies

· 201 ·

Someone greeting you with a huge,
beaming smile at the airport gate
after a terrible and tiresome trip

Life Is Good

· 202 ·

Fresh pajamas and some cushy
slippers to crawl into at night

· 203 ·

The solitary quiet
that unfolds as you sit in
your spiritual place

· 204 ·

Unwinding after a bad
day by reading mindless
fashion magazines

· 205 ·

The clacking of lacrosse
players' sticks on the field
on a cold fall afternoon

· 206 ·

Letting snowflakes
fall on your tongue

· 207 ·

Flipping a pancake out
of the pan and up in the air
and having it smack perfectly
back down on its other side

Life Is Good

· 208 ·

The cute way dogs circle
three times before they lie
down in their bed for a nap

· 209 ·

Those restaurants where you
get to color on the tablecloth

· 210 ·

Quiet walks through museum halls,
stopping occasionally to look at
something that calls out to you

Life Is Good

· 211 ·

The Road Runner's "Beep! Beep!"

· 212 ·

The contagious giggling
among friends that typically
occurs late at night

· 213 ·

Sumptuous bites of fresh peach
pie à la mode dangling
off your fork

Life Is Good

· 214 ·

Zoo animals that throw
caution to the wind and indulge
in a little romance in full view
of a growing audience

· 215 ·

Butter-soaked lobster tail

· 216 ·

The squeaks and creaks
emanating from the arm of an
old-fashioned water pump

· 217 ·

The traditional shaves still
possible at old-fashioned barber
establishments, with the old
proprietor slathering your neck
with hot shaving cream and
delicately trimming you down
with a perfectly sharp blade

· 218 ·

The delicate weight
and feel of a down
comforter at night

Life Is Good

· 219 ·

Beautiful planter boxes hanging
from windows that are alive with
flowing ivy and vibrant flowers

· 220 ·

The giddiness of finding an
English TV station while
you're traveling abroad

· 221 ·

The act of smoothing
hair back into a ponytail

Life Is Good

· 222 ·

Creamy and cool
Neosporin on a cut

· 223 ·

Walking into a movie theater with a
big bag of buttery good popcorn and
a *huge* lemonade that is certain to
make you run to the bathroom at
least once before the credits roll

· 224 ·

Touching rosary beads
and rolling them in your hand

· 225 ·

Being instantly
seated in a restaurant

· 226 ·

The excellent free food at
the office created by the budding
chef in your department

· 227 ·

The delicious nature of a deep
nap on your bed taken right after
an *exhausting* day of pool lounging
and sunning outdoors

· 228 ·

Slurps of cold water
straight from a garden hose

· 229 ·

Popcorn that is cooked right on
the stovetop and the wonderful
scratching sound of the pot being
rubbed against the stove eye

· 230 ·

The paradise the voice of Ella
Fitzgerald creates in your mind

Life Is Good

· 231 ·

The scratchy sound an old-fashioned
record makes as you place the
needle down for its first song

· 232 ·

Rose-scented drawer liners
that keep lingerie fresh

· 233 ·

Rubbing the cool and jiggly
belly of a Beluga whale at
San Antonio's Seaworld

Life Is Good

· 234 ·

Feather dusters

· 235 ·

Hearing the clacking
footsteps of a child in
plastic-footed pajamas

· 236 ·

Sesame Street's
theme music

Life Is Good

· 237 ·

The smell of a big
patch of lavender wafting over
from the neighbor's yard

· 238 ·

The sparkling look
of a just-scrubbed house

· 239 ·

"Chopsticks" played
on the piano

Life Is Good

• 240 •

Photographs that capture
the graceful tilt of a monarch
butterfly's wings and face

• 241 •

The funny tickle of rolling your
tummy with a lint roller to remove
the cat hair from your shirt

• 242 •

Lotion and cuticle cream
generously rubbed onto your
fingertips and palms

Life Is Good

· 243 ·

The soft, soothing
murmurs of a group reciting
a prayer in unison

· 244 ·

The eager drive home from
work on Friday afternoons

· 245 ·

Merry-go-round rides on the zany
Dr. Seuss-themed "Caro-Seuss-el" at
Universal's Islands of Adventure
theme park in Orlando

· 246 ·

Snow crunching under
your winter boots

· 247 ·

The electricity of being with
a great dancer on the floor when
you're both hitting the moves

· 248 ·

The sound of a golf ball
falling into the plastic hole
at the Putt-Putt course

· 249 ·

A litter of baby basset hounds
tripping over one another's
oversized ears while at play

· 250 ·

Really dressy hats
on good-looking women

· 251 ·

Warm coziness provided by just
the right amount of sun hitting
your back on the beach as you
let yourself bake a bit

· 252 ·

Evening walks

· 253 ·

The polka dancing, ale drinking,
and spicy bratwurst of a good
Wurstfest with friends in
New Braunfels, Texas

· 254 ·

Elvis impersonators—their lip
curling and exaggerated hip
swaggering is too delicious

· 255 ·

The satisfying sound
of a nutcracker successfully
popping open a walnut

· 256 ·

Miss Piggy's pretentiousness

Life Is Good

· 257 ·

The irreproducible smell
of banana nut bread made from
scratch baking in the oven

· 258 ·

The moment of quiet
before a kiss

· 259 ·

The magical dance of a sea horse
delicately fanning its fins

· 260 ·

Simple pepperoni pizza with
extra cheese on thin crust

· 261 ·

"Blue Hawaii" as sung by Willie
Nelson (and of course his classic,
"Always on My Mind")

Life Is Good

· 262 ·

The hum of the ice cream
machine as you swirl together
your own ice cream cone or
sundae at a buffet restaurant

· 263 ·

Alfred Hitchcock movies, specifically
The Birds and *Rear Window*

· 264 ·

The way your fingertips
get wet with milk when
you dunk Oreos

Life Is Good

· 265 ·

Hearing your beloved critter
come in through the pet door

· 266 ·

Rolling a perfume bottle's ball
over the arc of your wrist as the
scent rises up to your nose

· 267 ·

The delicate and perfect
feel of pink hydrangea
blossoms brushing against
the palm of your hand

• 268 •

How your breath transforms
into magical cloud puffs
when it's cold outside during
your morning walks

• 269 •

The sound of cracking eggs

• 270 •

Tissues with lanolin

· 271 ·

A duck's quack

· 272 ·

The way fireplace heat
warms your back

Life Is Good

· 273 ·

The cleansing feel
of sauna-induced sweating

· 274 ·

Quiet drives in the car
with both the radio and the
cell phone turned off—they
let your mind wander

· 275 ·

Granola cereal's perfect
crunch between your teeth

• 276 •

The smiling faces that peek
around the corner of your hospital
room door, asking if it's okay
to come in and visit

• 277 •

The click of a red plastic
View-Master flipping
to its next picture

• 278 •

Piano music—any kind

Life Is Good

· 279 ·

Homemade carrot cake that
is ultra-moist in your mouth

· 280 ·

Arguments about who
gets to lick the mixer's
chocolate-covered beaters

· 281 ·

The artistry of quilts expertly
made by the Amish, all spread
out on a country lawn for sale

Life Is Good

· 282 ·

The wisps of powder you
blow up as you "ride the lightning"
down a ski slope

· 283 ·

The deep level of pensiveness
that unfolds as you drive
at night down long and
uneventful interstate routes

· 284 ·

Popping bubbles floating
in the air with a fingertip

· 285 ·

A tea kettle sounding
from the kitchen stove

· 286 ·

Cat whiskers rubbing and
scenting against your legs

· 287 ·

The funny buzzing sound
when you make a mistake in
the board game "Operation"

Life Is Good

· 288 ·

Seeing loving couples
become bashful and red-faced
as they exchange wedding
vows on the big day

· 289 ·

Running your fingertip
along the lip of a glass bottle

· 290 ·

Throwing strands of silver
tinsel on a Christmas tree
to finish off its decoration

· 291 ·

Vigorous loofah scrubbings
on your back and elbows
in a super-hot shower

· 292 ·

Cool water from a spring-fed
well outside a cave in the
middle of nowhere in
Tennessee—nature's
unadulterated best

• 293 •

The metallic pop when you
open a tin of cookies or popcorn

• 294 •

That moment when the fish
you've caught first comes splashing
from the lake water and is visible
at the end of your line

• 295 •

Altoids mint therapy:
instant fresh mouth

· 296 ·

Soothing mental calm
that comes from performing
manual tasks like counting coins,
folding towels, or washing dishes

· 297 ·

The tune of a music box slowly
winding down, the metal teeth
sounding off the last few notes
against the cylinder inside

• 298 •

The clean smell of clothing
or sheets dried the
old-fashioned way
out on the line

• 299 •

Mickey Mouse's gloved hands

• 300 •

New babies looking cute and
wrinkly while layered in cotton
blankets behind the maternity
ward's clear windows

Life Is Good

· 301 ·

Goat's milk

· 302 ·

The light feeling of your
head after a haircut

· 303 ·

The little piles of shavings
left by men whittling sticks of
wood with their pocketknives

• 304 •

The chic way you look and
feel the split second after
you've finished getting
dressed up to go the theater
or a wedding—right before
you start mussing it all up!

• 305 •

Your cat touching noses with
you in the night and giving you
a tickle with her whiskers

· 306 ·

The steamy moist white
washcloths you get on airplanes
(and at some restaurants) to freshen
your hands and face with

· 307 ·

Those convoluted and
humorous "insert Tab A into Tab B"
directions that still have you
both stumped at 1 A.M.

· 308 ·

The colorful apparel of surfers

Life Is Good

· 309 ·

The rhythmic clicking of a
woman's high heels on a wood
floor or cement sidewalk

· 310 ·

Lying down on freshly
laid carpet and taking a good
strong whiff of its newness

· 311 ·

Thick, rich ketchup

· 312 ·

The sneaky-feeling fun
of peeing in the woods

· 313 ·

Sailing on the ocean water—
winding the ropes as fast as you
can and hearing the sails snap
in the gusts of the salty wind

· 314 ·

The silence between two
chess aficionados at war

• 315 •

The soft chiming of a
clock striking the hour

• 316 •

The all-enveloping peace and
comfort of knowing someone
is looking out for you

• 317 •

Swimming at nighttime in the
darkness and admiring the stars
while floating in the water

Life Is Good

• 318 •

The true miracle that is a baby
coming into the world with all ten
fingers and toes and all systems go

• 319 •

Feel and sound of a slick silk tie as
you fasten it around a man's neck

• 320 •

Turning a corner in a hyper-urban
area to see a lush floral stand
full of sunflowers, calla lilies, and
stalks of purple delphinium

· 321 ·

Rubbing a cold, perspiring
soda can against your head
when it's hot outside

· 322 ·

The pleasure of hearing a loved
one's car pulling into the driveway

· 323 ·

The secretive fun of sending and
receiving lovey-dovey e-mails to
break up the course of the workday

· 324 ·

The childish excitement
you still feel when you
unwrap a present by tearing
away at the taped corners
of the gift paper

· 325 ·

The rich, spicy smells of a
gentleman's smoking pipe and
how it dangles from his lips

Life Is Good

· 326 ·

Steamed milk from Starbucks

· 327 ·

Computer games like
Monkey Island, Quake, or
Sam and Max you can play
with a group of friends

· 328 ·

All the hysterical local
weirdoes you can laugh at on the
cable company's public-access
stations in the wee hours

Life Is Good

• 329 •

Leisurely weekend
champagne brunches

• 330 •

Women who don't wear make-up

• 331 •

Humongous closets

• 332 •

The tickle of misting yourself down
with bug spray at a cookout

Life Is Good

· 333 ·

The ritual of
smelling wine corks

· 334 ·

Braiding cornrows or pigtails
in a young girl's hair

· 335 ·

Warm glazed doughnuts

Life Is Good

• 336 •

Blowing balloons up and
feeling the round shape form
in the palm of your hand

• 337 •

The pleasantly sloshy
heft of a water balloon

• 338 •

There are people who
would travel thousands
of miles just to see you

Life Is Good

• 339 •

Birthday cards that come on time

• 340 •

Hurricanes on Bourbon Street
in New Orleans after a huge
bowl of spicy étoufée

• 341 •

The endorphin rushes
of early morning runs on
deserted sidewalks

Life Is Good

· 342 ·

The creamy tan foam atop a root
beer float in summertime

· 343 ·

All the writings of
Jane Austen, but specifically
Pride and Prejudice

· 344 ·

Giddily packing a suitcase for
the much-anticipated trip to
Florence, Italy, or anyplace
else you're raring to visit

Life Is Good

· 345 ·

The meticulous deliberations
around the wine rack concerning
what would best go with
chicken fettuccine alfredo

· 346 ·

Steaming hot chocolate on cold days

· 347 ·

Finding serenity in a brisk
thirty-minute walk in the city park
when your mind is troubled

· 348 ·

The friendly neighbor who
kindly removes the tarantula
from your garage without
thinking twice about it

· 349 ·

The funny way kids
misspell words in letters to
you (e.g., "You need to use
a see-*threw* glass.")

Life Is Good

• 350 •

The Eagles Greatest Hits CD

• 351 •

Gnawing on a straw that's
poking out of your glass

• 352 •

The warm colors and
aroma of a sampler platter
full of ales and lagers at the
brewery you're visiting

· 353 ·

Leisurely wrapping a gift for a
baby shower and smelling the tape
as you snap it off the dispenser
and hearing the crinkling of the
gift paper under your fingertips

· 354 ·

The ride home from the pound or
breeder where you have selected a
pet who now sits in the backseat
giving you love-y eyes and
radiating excitement

• 355 •

The rich smell when you open the
doors of the best pizza parlors

• 356 •

The special style you have for
attacking Reese's Cups

• 357 •

The clinking of ice
cubes in a glass

· 358 ·

Comedy club evenings where the
comedian picks on the people in the
front row in between sips from his
water bottle and his eye-rolling

· 359 ·

The feel of an arm around your waist
as you navigate a slippery surface

· 360 ·

Watching butterflies flitter
about in the garden

• 361 •

The dramatic red of a ruby

• 362 •

Cathartic nature of
hammering a nail into the
wall for a picture

• 363 •

Your collection of birthday or "just
because" greeting cards you've
received over the years

Life Is Good

· 364 ·

The rugged hymns you still hear
in remote country churches, like
"Will the Circle Be Unbroken"

· 365 ·

The relief of waking from
a nightmare and realizing
none of it was real

· 366 ·

The trance you fall into on bus rides
from the soothing motion of slow
travel and unhurried stops and starts

Life Is Good

· 367 ·

The crunch of
perfectly crisp toast

· 368 ·

Leprechauns

· 369 ·

The snap! snap!
of the clipper at work on
your finger- and toenails

Life Is Good

· 370 ·

The taste of the syrup left at the
bottom of the banana split tray

· 371 ·

The feel of the warm wax that
you intentionally spill out of the
candle to mold and play with

· 372 ·

Chicken salad that is packed
with walnuts and celery pieces and
served atop a crisp croissant

Life Is Good

· 373 ·

The way cats "knead dough"
on your tummy when you
come in from work

· 374 ·

Smeared butter on
top of hot apple bread

· 375 ·

The special magic that first
moment the Christmas lights are
turned on in the winter season

Life Is Good

· 376 ·

Sunrays bouncing off lake water

· 377 ·

The magic and perfect warmth
of a bonfire with friends

· 378 ·

The feel of popcorn crumbs and
butter on your fingertips

· 379 ·

Swishing a fleshy green
grape in your mouth with your
tongue and pressing it against
the back of your teeth

· 380 ·

The smell of salt water
that starts sneaking into your
car a few miles before you actually
make it to the beach

Life Is Good

· 381 ·

The taste of warm crunchy pumpkin
seeds just plucked from pumpkins
and roasted in the oven with
sprinkles of Lawry's Seasoned Salt

· 382 ·

The perfect crease you make
in the spine of a paperback novel
when you prepare to read it

· 383 ·

Popping your knuckles and
joints with a good stretch

· 384 ·

Curling up in a chenille throw
on the couch while watching
"Must-See TV" on Thursday night

· 385 ·

Dunking dainty butter cookies into
a steaming cup of chamomile tea

· 386 ·

When someone's nails
adroitly attack the spot that's
itching on your back

Life Is Good

· 387 ·

Tick-tocking of an antique
grandfather clock

· 388 ·

Your instant excitement when
you smell your favorite food cooking
on the stove and then take a
moment to give it an extra stir

· 389 ·

The rough tongue of a cat giving
your elbow a bit of grooming

Life Is Good

· 390 ·

The light feel of a patch of
dandelions under your hand

· 391 ·

Semi-dissolved saltine crackers
in chicken noodle soup

· 392 ·

Soft-serve chocolate
ice cream in crunchy cones

Life Is Good

• 393 •

The feel of a flower
petal in your palm

• 394 •

The arch in
Jack Nicholson's eyebrows

• 395 •

The flapping sound
of opening a crisp and clean
dinner napkin as you prepare
for dinner at a restaurant

· 396 ·

The cute roundness
of your pregnant friends

· 397 ·

The way the Icee or Slurpee
gushes out from the machine
at the convenience mart

· 398 ·

Watching sunset unfold
with someone you love

Life Is Good

· 399 ·

All laughter in the
company of friends

· 400 ·

The feel of silky
pajamas under your hand
at Victoria's Secret

· 401 ·

The loud lapping
of a dog at its water bowl
on a hot day

· 402 ·

The light tugs on your scalp
as someone braids your hair

· 403 ·

A bowl of steaming
chili swimming with
crunchy Fritos chips

· 404 ·

A wine glass with just the right
weight and feel in your hand

Life Is Good

· 405 ·

Scrambled eggs and buttered
toast at the Waffle House

· 406 ·

Little yellow rubber
duckies floating in
a tub of bath water

Life Is Good

· 407 ·

The trademark sound of
flip-flops smacking against
your feet as you stroll along
sidewalks in the summertime

· 408 ·

*It's the Great Pumpkin,
Charlie Brown*

· 409 ·

Watching three golden lab puppies
play tug of war with every shoe that
has not been put away in the closet

· 410 ·

Lilac trees unfurling
their purple flowers in spring
and inundating the yard with
a tender, sweet smell

· 411 ·

The energy surrounding football
games between great rivals

· 412 ·

The loving way you treasure your
very first business card

Life Is Good

· 413 ·

The "You want to eat everything
we have now" smell that wafts
from the doors of tucked away,
mom-'n'-pop doughnut bakeries

· 414 ·

The squeaking sound of wiping
Windex off the bathroom mirror

· 415 ·

The cheery clusters
of white and red poinsettias
around the holidays

• 416 •

The delicate smell of
Baby Magic Baby Wash being
squirted out of its bottle

• 417 •

The calming act of floating on your
back at the ocean or a pool

• 418 •

The sound and smell
of bicycle tires working
on wet pavement

Life Is Good

· 419 ·

The serenity of watching
leaves swirl around in
eddies of wind

· 420 ·

Laughing about old
worries that never surfaced
as you review your past

· 421 ·

The clacking of plastic
chopsticks over your fried rice

Life Is Good

· 422 ·

Laughing so hard you have
to double over to discourage
the desire to snort for air

· 423 ·

The ripple in the field
of wheat caused by the
winds before harvest time

· 424 ·

The smell of a black leather
jacket and gloves you wear
in crisp fall weather

· 425 ·

The wonderfully cute
nose of the pig

· 426 ·

The goofy sense of camaraderie
you feel when you pass a driver
on the road who has a car the
same make, model, and color
as your own—you almost
feel obligated to roll down
the window and say,
"Let's do coffee!"

· 427 ·

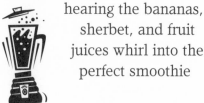

Pushing the blender buttons and hearing the bananas, sherbet, and fruit juices whirl into the perfect smoothie

· 428 ·

A rainbow arch appearing to celebrate the end of a spring shower

Life Is Good

· 429 ·

Getting a postcard
from a foreign country
with its unusual stamp
and tattered appearance

· 430 ·

The pleasant surprise
of finding money or other
treasures in the pockets
of a jacket you haven't
worn in a while

Life Is Good

· 431 ·

The velveteen muzzle
of a horse brushing your hand
as you feed it crunchy corn

· 432 ·

The way children
rub their eyes with their
knuckles when they are
very sleepy and yawning

· 433 ·

How fast Hot Wheels
cars glide across tile floors

Life Is Good

· 434 ·

The pleasant percussion
of a storm's raindrops
pelting the windows

· 435 ·

A huge, golden moon
hanging in a fall sky

· 436 ·

The near-invisible beating
of a tiny hummingbird's
wings in flight

Life Is Good

· 437 ·

The smell of fresh
pine needles

· 438 ·

A field of bluebonnets
covering a field in a Texas spring

· 439 ·

The texture of real
butter that's been left out
to soften before dinner

Life Is Good

· 440 ·

The proud feeling right after
you've managed to skillfully
avoid hitting an animal that was
hesitantly crossing the road

· 441 ·

The snapping of breaking
fresh green beans in halves

· 442 ·

The magical feeling of
a pregnant woman's swollen
tummy under your fingertips

Life Is Good

· 443 ·

Meticulously picking and
choosing which flowers will
compose a bouquet, either at the
florist or in the rose garden

· 444 ·

Huge, plastic
rainbow-colored
beach ball

· 445 ·

A fresh coat of
white paint on the wall

• 446 •

Pulling your hat down
low over your eyes and taking
in a catnap while sunning at
the pool on a chaise lounge

• 447 •

The sound of water
rising to a vigorous boil

• 448 •

The pleasure of plumping up your
feather pillow by patting the ends
before you let your head sink into it

Life Is Good

· 449 ·

The proud, taut muscles
of a black Tennessee walking
horse trotting around a show
ring with its signature gait

· 450 ·

The grace and strength
of a solid golf swing (Tiger Woods's
always comes to mind.)

· 451 ·

The spinning of a
potter's wheel in motion

· 452 ·

Hearing the pop of fresh toast
launching from the toaster

· 453 ·

Watching geese fly in
"V" formation high above
your head while you pause
from raking the orange and
red leaves at your feet

· 454 ·

The "smart" smell of a bookstore

Life Is Good

· 455 ·

Watching the perfect white tips of a
French manicure being painted on

· 456 ·

Comfy denim overalls

· 457 ·

How hot beverages
perfectly warm your throat
and stomach in cold weather

Life Is Good

· 458 ·

The clacking sound of a plastic
Trivial Pursuit game piece being
moved around the board

· 459 ·

The sensation created
from a dream in which
you can fly

· 460 ·

The freedom to
express yourself

· 461 ·

"Dancer's high"—the sweet
rush you get in the middle
of a night of boogying
with a group of buddies

· 462 ·

The theme music that
precedes Bugs Bunny cartoons—
On with the show, this is it!

· 463 ·

Yodeling

· 464 ·

Warm crepes filled with
creamy Nutella chocolate spread
and fresh banana slices

· 465 ·

The super-clean feel of
a mouth freshly flossed

· 466 ·

The way ice cream sandwiches
dissolve so well on your tongue,
the chocolate wafer only thinly
protecting the ice cream

Life Is Good

· 467 ·

The heavenly feel
of your own bed after
a week in a hotel

· 468 ·

The special magic
of a vertical rainbow

· 469 ·

The way your furry
slippers protect you from
the cold kitchen floor

· 470 ·

Scattering bread or grains
on the sidewalk at the park
and watching the birds
cluster around for the feast

· 471 ·

Warm brownies with
walnuts fresh from the oven
and superbly cold milk

· 472 ·

Those moments when
you become totally cool,
calm, and collected under
pressure and are overcome
with the proud realization
that you are, in fact,
James Bond

· 473 ·

Cartoon Network
marathons

· 474 ·

The primitive pleasure
of eating a boiled egg by sucking
and biting on its smaller end

· 475 ·

Big bouquets of
multicolored balloons

Life Is Good

· 476 ·

Any *Curious George* book

· 477 ·

The thumping sounds of a
ten-pound cat running wild through
the house while high on catnip

· 478 ·

The perfect last bite of an ice cream
cone, consisting of the softened
bottom of the cone that melts in your
mouth due to its sustained contact
with your scoop of chocolate mint

Life Is Good

· 479 ·

Little toddlers at swimming pools
who wear those orange floaters that
prop their arms up all akimbo

· 480 ·

Watching the Olympics with friends
while surrounded with lots of
crunchy junk foods and sodas

· 481 ·

Cushy oven mitts covering both
your hands as you pull out a hot
cookie sheet full of goodies

Life Is Good

· 482 ·

Cherry Kool-Aid

· 483 ·

The giraffe—you just gotta laugh
when you really look at one

· 484 ·

The crunchy sound of
packing snowballs together
while forming the perfect
snowman in the front yard

· 485 ·

The way kids create "forts" and
"tents" in their room by spreading
and hanging blankets from their
bedposts and dresser tops

· 486 ·

The way the kitchen
counter of a passionate
cook always becomes
splattered and covered with
a myriad of flour and spices
during the creation of pasta
dishes from scratch

· 487 ·

The Beatles' *One* CD

· 488 ·

Wearing ragged, beloved
T-shirts that should be thrown
out but that you can't bear to
part with because they are
so soft against your skin

· 489 ·

Saturday Night Live

Life Is Good

· 490 ·

All the wonderful toys,
games, and candies at
FAO Schwartz toy stores

· 491 ·

Shooting stars in a Texas
sky during a midnight dog walk

· 492 ·

The whir of a fishing
reel as you cast the line
across the water

· 493 ·

Murder on the Orient Express
and *Ten Little Indians*
by Agatha Christie

· 494 ·

The heavy feel of a faithful
handmade quilt as you nestle
beneath its warmth

· 495 ·

That lusciously moist Black Forest
cake you can get at food stands
in the streets of Vienna

· 496 ·

The feel of sliding on your favorite
pair of blue jeans—they just
magically adhere to your body

· 497 ·

Clean powdery baby smell

Life Is Good

· 498 ·

Peeling the paper off
a new bar of soap and taking
in the clean smell

· 499 ·

The pleasant way bubbles
break the surface of tomato
sauce as it simmers

· 500 ·

The crunch of biting into
a caramel, nut-covered apple
at a school carnival

· 501 ·

The unbelievable spectacle
of a Cirque Du Soleil show—the
strength, agility, and sheer athletic
prowess of the performers can
inspire you to start doing your
Abs of Steel tape again

· 502 ·

The occasional, delightful
find of a group of tadpoles
in a puddle or stream

· 503 ·

The momentary, if silly,
excitement of finding you
have a message on your
answering machine

· 504 ·

The velvet touch of a stingray's
body in warm Grand Cayman
waters (They're like big velvet
pancakes, and they'll suck bits
of squid out of your hand if
you have a delicate approach.)

Life Is Good

· 505 ·

Dunkin' Donuts
chocolate Munchkins

· 506 ·

The bigger, cushier,
Lazy Boy-esque chairs of
modern movie theaters

· 507 ·

Cheesy game shows like
The Price Is Right, Family Feud,
and *Wheel of Fortune*

Life Is Good

· 508 ·

Digging into your arm muscles with
a strong muscle cream after a day
spent canoeing in Arkansas

· 509 ·

The perfect crease
of your worn wallet

· 510 ·

A boat ride across the sea
where you can watch mist spring
from the bow and point at
dolphin fins on the horizon

Life Is Good

· 511 ·

Scooby Doo's voice ("Ruby-roo?")

· 512 ·

The striking red of
a bullfighter's blanket

· 513 ·

The comforting feel of your
watch on your wrist—most
appreciated on those days when
you forget it on the dresser

Life Is Good

• 514 •

Pulpy orange juice
rolling across your tongue

• 515 •

Prolonging your departure
to work by slowly stirring
your second coffee and enjoying
the more obscure sections
of the morning paper

Life Is Good

· 516 ·

The delicate artistry and amazing
complexity of the honeycomb
floating in your honey jar

· 517 ·

Competitive round of *Monopoly*,
where hotels on Park Place and
Boardwalk are a true coup

· 518 ·

The delectably light flavor of a
super-fresh piece of sushi, be it
yellowtail or a wimpy California roll

· 519 ·

The emotional rush
of the last pages of the
amazing novels that have
truly touched your soul

· 520 ·

The occasional find
of an old-fashioned soda
machine where you can still
get little baby bottles of Coke

Life Is Good

· 521 ·

The nervous excitement of the
first day of school, whether it's the
third grade or graduate studies

· 522 ·

The springy metallic sound
of the beloved Slinky

· 523 ·

The sight of a spinning
world globe in a classroom

Life Is Good

· 524 ·

The first tip of a green
stalk that emerges from
a gnarled, brown iris bulb

· 525 ·

Spider webs sprinkled with dew

· 526 ·

Bites of ultra-cheesy authentic
deep-dish pizza in Chicago

Life Is Good

· 527 ·

The shimmer off the bubble
just set free from the wand
an inch from your lips

· 528 ·

The fascinating way a
caterpillar slowly inches along
toward its destination

· 529 ·

The sound of a sticker
being pulled from its sheet

· 530 ·

Boys and girls in
those tennis shoes that
showcase blinky red
lights when they run

· 531 ·

Eating creamy spinach dip
on the balcony of a
beachfront restaurant and
taking in a gorgeous Del
Mar sunset (Thanks, Kathy.)

Life Is Good

· 532 ·

Those perfect outdoor
tables on the patio of a restaurant
overlooking a lake

· 533 ·

Finishing off the sweet-smelling,
drippy cake batter you scraped off
the bottom of the mixing bowl

· 534 ·

Those great New York City–style
hot dogs smothered with
mustard and sauerkraut

Life Is Good

· 535 ·

Playing with airy bread
dough with your fingertips, leaving
those cute dimple marks

· 536 ·

The way a dog's face totally
lights up when you say the
word "walk" or "treat"

· 537 ·

Shuffling cards and feeling them
fold up under your hand before you
deal a round of five-card stud

· 538 ·

Visiting someone who still cans food
and studying the beautiful, colorful
culinary creations in mason jars
perched on her countertop

· 539 ·

The original *Star Wars* trilogy and
absolutely anything related to it

· 540 ·

The way change
jingles in a mason jar

· 541 ·

The intricate beauty
of a snake's scales

· 542 ·

The deliciously
pleasant way your stylist
massages shampoo into
your scalp and hair

Life Is Good

· 543 ·

Moist coconut cake
that just dissolves on your
tongue, sugary-sweet

· 544 ·

Those toy mice cats
love that have loud beads
rattling inside them

· 545 ·

Reflections of sky and clouds
in all the puddles you walk
by after a rainstorm

· 546 ·

Indulging in people
watching from a bench
at the plaza, sipping on
a cup of coffee and
appreciating the breezes

· 547 ·

Blowing air through
your straw to make some more
bubbles in your Sprite

Life Is Good

· 548 ·

The fresh feeling of splashing
water on your face in the morning
and at the close of the day

· 549 ·

Pounding darts into a dartboard
at your favorite Irish pub

· 550 ·

Squeezing a lemon wedge
into your iced tea and plopping
it into your glass

· 551 ·

Pulling the tag off a Hershey's Kiss
and hearing the foil come loose

· 552 ·

The free therapy provided by
scrubbing a car in the driveway with
a fat sopping sponge and then drying
it well with a smooth chamois

· 553 ·

The chugging sounds coming
from an inverted water bottle
you're taking huge gulps from

Life Is Good

· 554 ·

Slicing apples on the cutting
board and getting out the salt
shaker from the cupboard

· 555 ·

Walking through the water-misting
stations amusement parks set
up to combat the summer heat

· 556 ·

Rich home-brewed beer
that actually tastes good

· 557 ·

The clop-clopping of horses
traveling on pavement in a parade

· 558 ·

The feeling that overtakes
you when realizing how much
you truly love someone

· 559 ·

Feeling the sturdy bark
under your hands when
you climb a tree

· 560 ·

The clicking of the gumball
machine's handle when you turn it
for a treat, and the rattling of the
surprise rolling out to you

· 561 ·

Peaceful strolls around
a golf course's well-manicured
greens with clubs in hand

· 562 ·

The giddy tingle you get
hotrodding with the rental car
you were overcharged for

· 563 ·

Heartily slurping through a straw
when no one else is around

· 564 ·

The feel of those wonderfully light
green baskets that strawberries are
packaged in at the grocery store

Life Is Good

· 565 ·

James Taylor singing
"Fire and Rain"

· 566 ·

Heating blankets on
the highest setting

· 567 ·

The fun of setting out all the
things on the bed as you decide
what to take on a trip

Life Is Good

· 568 ·

The old episodes
of *Scooby Doo* where the
Harlem Globetrotters visit

· 569 ·

The crackle of wood
burning in the fireplace

· 570 ·

Sliding watermelon seeds
around in your mouth before you
spit them onto the grass

· 571 ·

The grainy feel of wash
detergent in your palm

· 572 ·

A pink amaryllis on the
very verge of blooming

· 573 ·

The comforting buzz
and rhythmic stitching of a
sewing machine hard at work

Life Is Good

• 574 •

A fresh waffle cone filled
with a double scoop of
butter pecan ice cream

• 575 •

The way cats lay in patches
of afternoon sun creeping
through the windows

• 576 •

The surreal quality of waking up
in the wee hours because coyotes
are howling in the distance

Life Is Good

· 577 ·

The feel of the worn silky
quilt that has traveled with
you since childhood

· 578 ·

The delightful smell of basil and
parsley growing in the kitchen
window sill above the sink

· 579 ·

Looking at your blue tongue
in the mirror after you've
drunk a blue cherry Icee

· 580 ·

The fun of observing *totally*
passionate cooks at work and
witnessing their seriousness about
the difference between pure olive
oil and extra virgin olive oil

· 581 ·

The clickety-clack of a dog's feet
trotting across a tile floor

· 582 ·

Cape Canaveral shuttle launches

Life Is Good

· 583 ·

Bouncy piggy-back rides

· 584 ·

Sliding around in socks
on freshly waxed and
slick hardwood floors

· 585 ·

The oozy goodness of a
warm Taco Bell bean burrito

Life Is Good

· 586 ·

The smooth touch of a brown
rabbit sniffing your outstretched
fingers in search of a carrot

· 587 ·

Seriously frosted
mugs full of Corona

· 588 ·

The clicking sounds
from stacking Lincoln Logs
atop one another

· 589 ·

Secretly talking and
whispering to your
stuffed animals

· 590 ·

Pressing down the clutch
when you shift to fifth gear

Life Is Good

· 591 ·

Bazooka gum cartoons

· 592 ·

Twisting the stick you've
covered with marshmallows
over a spitting fire and waiting
for the perfect blackening

· 593 ·

Clifford the Big Red Dog

Life Is Good

• 594 •

The squeak of windshield wipers

• 595 •

Slurping on a Capri Sun bag

• 596 •

Super-smooth and cold
Noxzema tingling your cheeks

• 597 •

Flower pollen coating your
fingertips after a visit to the garden

· 598 ·

The camaraderie of friends
trying to create the perfect
salmon pasta sauce on the
stove despite the effects
of plenty of Chianti

· 599 ·

Falling into the snow off your
skis or a sled and feeling the
sensation of cold, not the actual
moisture or dampness, filter
through your slick gloves
and snowsuit bottom

Life Is Good

· 600 ·

The loud, yet majestic,
flapping of a huge flag
unfurled in high winds

· 601 ·

Fences absolutely *covered*
with honeysuckle vines

· 602 ·

Labrador retrievers playing
fetch in cold weather with their
collar tags jingling as they romp

· 603 ·

Letters from children away
at camp that contain pressed
leaves and flowers

· 604 ·

The electricity that
builds in a band and crowd
at a really great concert

· 605 ·

Cannonball dives
into the swimming pool

Life Is Good

· 606 ·

Swishing sounds from a woman
walking by in a formal gown

· 607 ·

Peeling up a page from the
day-by-day calendar on your desk

· 608 ·

Streakers

· 609 ·

The theme music of Tetris

Life Is Good

· 610 ·

The comfortable feel
of chewing on a toothpick

· 611 ·

Yelling "UNO!"

· 612 ·

The humorous way a cat
meticulously and cautiously
approaches something
it wants to investigate

Life Is Good

• 613 •

Sonic limeades

• 614 •

The feel of an old text in an
antiquarian bookstore

• 615 •

Jingling of Christmas
bells attached to a door

Life Is Good

· 616 ·

The ritual of lightly
brushing on mascara

· 617 ·

Stolen slurps straight
out of the milk jug

Life Is Good

· 618 ·

Letting tall plants brush
the palms of your hands
as you walk along

· 619 ·

Stepping onto the cushy bath
mat after a shower or bath

· 620 ·

Sinking into the plush
cushions and masculine smell
of a giant leather couch

Life Is Good

· 621 ·

The we-should-bottle-it-and-sell-it
luminescent look that new
parents bestow upon their
new family member

· 622 ·

The muffled sounds
in your submerged ears
as you snorkel along a coral
reef looking for lobsters

· 623 ·

A warm and furry cat wrapped
around your feet and ankles
during a cold, sleepy night

· 624 ·

The sheen on a new
pair of cowboy boots

· 625 ·

Pouring and dribbling sauces
and dressings just the way you
like on your pasta or salad

Life Is Good

· 626 ·

Having the perfect
godparents for your children

· 627 ·

Soothing Halls cough
drops for your raw throat

· 628 ·

Red fuzzy earmuffs

· 629 ·

The relaxation of
fingering the silky threads
composing a tassel

· 630 ·

The soothing and
regular tumbling sounds of
a clothes dryer at work

· 631 ·

The way diamonds sparkle

· 632 ·

People's funny poker-playing
rituals—like kissing the top of
the card deck before they deal
and insisting that honkey-tonk
be played as background music

· 633 ·

There still being some of those
kind folks out there who take
time to stop and give you very
detailed directions when you're
in the middle of nowhere and
have no idea where to go

• 634 •

The humor of "freeze head"

• 635 •

Buttery chocolate chip scones
that crumble in your mouth

• 636 •

The stores where you get
to build and customize your own
teddy bears and watch the
process of their creation

· 637 ·

The lightheartedness that comes
with gliding on ice skates

· 638 ·

The way the staff at your favorite
restaurant always smiles at you and
knows your order by heart

· 639 ·

The sticky notes from a treasured
coworker that say "Good luck!"
you find on your desk
occasionally before meetings

Life Is Good

· 640 ·

The pinging sound of Fruity
Pebbles cereal hitting the bowl

· 641 ·

Holding and admiring
a beautiful Wedgwood china plate

· 642 ·

Succumbing to the temptation
of a crunchy funnel cake
at the amusement park

Life Is Good

· 643 ·

The miraculous shapes
and brilliant colors of
fish scales and fins

· 644 ·

Sloppy wet dog
kisses on your hand

· 645 ·

There are still plenty
of men alive who proudly
wear lederhosen.

Life Is Good

• 646 •

The beautiful way the
bunches of green and red
grapes sparkle on the vine

• 647 •

The clipping sounds of
scissors slicing through paper

• 648 •

The ubiquitous Twinkie

· 649 ·

The way the sky is so open
in Texas when you look up to
study the stars or the clouds

· 650 ·

Ivy-covered college buildings—
they make you want to immediately
read a philosophy book

· 651 ·

Having Evian atomizers to
mist your face when you
require instant cool-downs

· 652 ·

Fudgsicles from the freezer that
are so cold they have little
patches of ice covering
the surface that you
can lick as well

· 653 ·

How gulls ride the breezes and hover
only feet away from the ocean water

· 654 ·

Cats attacking your wrapping
paper as you try to get a gift
put together on the floor

Life Is Good

• 655 •

Kermit's "The Rainbow
Connection" song

• 656 •

The ultra-moisturizing
feel of the suntan oil rubbed
onto your belly poolside

• 657 •

The ethereal unified voice of the
crowd at a concert when the
performers stop singing and
encourage the fans to finish a chorus

Life Is Good

· 658 ·

Running carefree through
sprinklers and getting
covered in tiny splatters

· 659 ·

Birds and squirrels humorously
hanging out on your patio chairs
as if they own the place

· 660 ·

The much-welcomed way you
cool down after throwing on a
stylish straw hat at the pool

Life Is Good

· 661 ·

Sincere and heartfelt charity

· 662 ·

The rush of moving into
a new home and getting to
decorate a fresh new space

· 663 ·

The PFFFSSS! of hair mousse
and shaving cream being
pumped out of their cans

· 664 ·

Funny little lap dogs
with cute faces that bark
as if they're rottweilers

· 665 ·

The joy of those special occasions
when you hit a string of all green
lights during your commute home

· 666 ·

The perfect chicken taco
at a tucked-away dive

Life Is Good

• 667 •

The exaggerated sense of
self-accomplishment you have when
you sew a button back on a shirt

• 668 •

Tubing trips down cool rivers where
you swat the top of the water with
your hands as you float along

• 669 •

The slap of a jump rope
against cement followed by the
rhythmic beat of a child's feet

Life Is Good

· 670 ·

Cartoon character-covered
Band-Aids—they're not
just for kids anymore

· 671 ·

Potpourri burners that fill rooms
with cinnamon or orange scents

· 672 ·

The sonorous tone in an airplane
that indicates you can get up and
finally go to the restroom

Life Is Good

· 673 ·

The time at the zoo
when you heard how thunderous
a lion's roar really is

· 674 ·

The sensation of someone
zipping or unzipping the back
of your outfit for you

· 675 ·

Squishing the warm collection
of lint in your hand that you just
pulled from the dryer's filter

· 676 ·

The mesmerizing way
rice absorbs soy sauce

· 677 ·

A French fry swabbed with
just the right amount of ketchup

· 678 ·

The way your muscles
tingle and burn after a really
good workout with weights

Life Is Good

· 679 ·

The amazing way totally
fat squirrels somehow manage
to still get into your strategically
placed birdfeeders

· 680 ·

Dennis Miller's laugh

· 681 ·

The relaxing and
deep sleep following an
A.M. romp with a lover

Life Is Good

· 682 ·

Rubbing your fingers
against the smooth, pearlescent
interior of a shell found
along the beach

· 683 ·

The mental break afforded
by doing some needlepoint

· 684 ·

Crunchy cucumbers
at the salad bar

Life Is Good

• 685 •

Globs inside lava lamps
floating about like ghosts

• 686 •

The sound of aluminum foil
being clipped by the serrated metal
cutter on the side of its box

• 687 •

Wrapping up in a
sun-baked towel after
emerging from a cold pool

· 688 ·

Dark German beers so thick and
brown you can't see through the
glasses they're served in

· 689 ·

Young trick-or-treaters bounding
around the neighborhood

Life Is Good

· 690 ·

Groups of shy,
grazing deer on the
roadside late at night

· 691 ·

The feel of washing your belly
button with a soft washcloth

· 692 ·

The flapping sounds
of a kite caught in
a good breeze

Life Is Good

· 693 ·

Peeling softened ice cream
out of the container
with a steel scooper

· 694 ·

The perfect square of comforting
warmth provided by your heating
pad when your tummy is ill

· 695 ·

Rising steam from a hot
tub in cold weather

Life Is Good

· 696 ·

The soft cushiness of a roll
of expensive toilet paper

· 697 ·

Rows of icicles suspended
from overhangs in winter

· 698 ·

Those deft servers at fine
restaurants who so gracefully
pour a steaming tea or coffee

Life Is Good

• 699 •

The seasoning honey-roasted
peanuts leave on your fingers
that you have to lick off

• 700 •

The drive across the causeway
connecting mainland Florida
with its beautiful Keys

• 701 •

The perfect sense of clean
in your mouth after a gargle
of Scope or Listerine

· 702 ·

The smooth lines of
a marble sculpture that you
can trace with a fingertip

· 703 ·

The neat look of the
vibration of a guitar string
strummed with a plastic pick

· 704 ·

The cool smoothness
of a feather boa

Life Is Good

· 705 ·

Nuzzling against a
soft beard or goatee

· 706 ·

The act of folding up
the newspaper page to
best get at the crossword

· 707 ·

The clacking of an air
hockey puck being tossed back
and forth in zesty competition

· 708 ·

Battered ornaments on Christmas
trees that obviously came from an
elementary school crafts class

· 709 ·

Twirling an umbrella in the rain

· 710 ·

Showers of white confetti

· 711 ·

The slick surface of dominoes

Life Is Good

· 712 ·

The whirring, wet sounds
of the dishwasher

· 713 ·

Mint-condition
baseball cards

· 714 ·

The shiny slickness
of faithful L. L. Bean
sleeping bags

· 715 ·

Perfect bubblegum bubbles
perched on your lips

· 716 ·

The way your skin
drinks in citrus-scented
lotion after a warm bath

· 717 ·

The tickle of crisp air against
your cheeks as you skate
or ski in the wintertime

· 718 ·

The crayon scent of most
elementary school classrooms

· 719 ·

Riding in a loud motorboat—
the noise prevents you from
speaking to anyone, so you
focus on the water and
sunlight surrounding you

Life Is Good

· 720 ·

The velveteen feel
of a dairy cow's udders

· 721 ·

Buttery, salted mall pretzels

· 722 ·

The Giving Tree—its shiny
cover still beckons from
shelves at every bookstore

Life Is Good

· 723 ·

The pleasant sound of
long hair being brushed

· 724 ·

How groups of people
do the universal moves of the
"YMCA" dance together

· 725 ·

The soft glow of
frosted light bulbs

Life Is Good

· 726 ·

The sneaky dolphins
that escape with the fish you
naively leave on a trout line

· 727 ·

The human blush

· 728 ·

The cadence of an old
man's cane moving across a
sidewalk or hardwood floor

· 729 ·

The sweet smell
of the rotisserie area of
any BBQ restaurant

· 730 ·

White Christmas lights

· 731 ·

Hearty pats on the back

Life Is Good

· 732 ·

The sound of pulling up
a Teva sandal's Velcro strap

· 733 ·

The artfully disguised
athleticism of a prima ballerina
in motion in her dainty dress

· 734 ·

Toddlers who are just figuring
out the dynamics of walking and
are thrilled with the discovery

· 735 ·

The traditional and
sturdy silver Thermos

· 736 ·

The squeaking of
balloons being twisted
into cute animal shapes

· 737 ·

The weight, feel, and curve
of your favorite ink pen gliding
smoothly across paper

· 738 ·

Mexican blankets

· 739 ·

Tylenol sinus medication

· 740 ·

Jimmy Buffet's "Margaritaville"

Life Is Good

· 741 ·

How the first bite of a meal
tastes when you're truly hungry
and needing calories

· 742 ·

Birds flitting about the
bird bath in hot weather

· 743 ·

McDonald's French fries

Life Is Good

· 744 ·

The humorous way that
babies and toddlers can't
seem to keep socks on

· 745 ·

The tapping sound of nimble
fingers on a computer keyboard

· 746 ·

Beautifully preserved or restored
Victorian homes with lots of white
gingerbread trim and big porches
with huge wicker chairs

· 747 ·

Fragrant white gardenias
contrasting beautifully against
their bright green foliage

· 748 ·

Seats on shaded, cool cement
during the summertime

· 749 ·

The rhythmic pounding of
a jogger hitting the pavement
in the wee hours

Life Is Good

· 750 ·

Beaches at night—they're cold as anything but the sight of moonlight on water and the continued sounds of surf can be too beautiful to leave

· 751 ·

"Hey Jude" by The Beatles

· 752 ·

The wave of your friendly neighbor

· 753 ·

A whole bag of chewy
taffy with your name on it

· 754 ·

The taste of snow

· 755 ·

The fun sound of cymbals
crashing together

Life Is Good

· 756 ·

Bottles of Dom Perignon
on special occasions

· 757 ·

The delicious ritual of
smacking on your bubble
gum while alone

Life Is Good

· 758 ·

The Little Leaguers who
proudly strut in their new
uniforms in the springtime

· 759 ·

The cream center
of a Ding Dong

· 760 ·

Quirky superstitions
like not stepping on
cracks and patting pregnant
women's bellies for luck

Life Is Good

· 761 ·

Baby chimpanzees rolling
around at the zoo

· 762 ·

The endorphin rush
provided by *ultra*-spicy foods
such as "fire in the hole"-flavored
buffalo wings, anything Thai,
and "five alarm" chili

· 763 ·

Soft hen's feathers
under your hand

· 764 ·

A row of little girls
in pink tutus

· 765 ·

The calming sounds
of water trickling
down a fountain

· 766 ·

All the speeding tickets
you should have gotten but didn't

· 767 ·

The steady tempo
of a person chopping up
firewood at a lodge

· 768 ·

Those kindly people
who say "Bless you"
after you sneeze

· 769 ·

Frostys from
Wendy's restaurants

· 770 ·

The familiar weight of your
pocketknife in your pants pocket

· 771 ·

The fact that Jim Henson
lived on this planet

· 772 ·

Those funny moments
when a giddy pet runs off
with something it *knows* it's
not supposed to have, like
a shoe or your bath loofah

· 773 ·

The pleasant tone of
the doorbell when you're
expecting a friend

· 774 ·

Those moments in team
sports where you and your
teammates are working in total
unity and understanding and
are completely in the zone

Life Is Good

· 775 ·

Real snow cones
where you attack the top
mound of ice with a
little plastic spoon

· 776 ·

The pleasant sounds
of getting dressed in the
morning: buttons snapping
together and zippers
humming to a close

Life Is Good

· 777 ·

The peaceful solitude
of standing on a bridge
and simply watching
water pass under you

· 778 ·

Swans elegantly
floating on water

· 779 ·

Those wonderful waiters
who go the extra mile to make
your dinner special

· 780 ·

The beauty of a
shimmering pearl

· 781 ·

Credence Clearwater
Revival singing "Proud Mary"

Life Is Good

· 782 ·

The hypnotic allure
of an empty bench
in a patch of green

· 783 ·

The fluid motions of
a sculptor's fingertips on her
current work in progress

· 784 ·

Warm tortillas

Life Is Good

· 785 ·

The sneaky rush of spitting
off a tall building

· 786 ·

Catching your
reflection in bubbles

· 787 ·

The snipping scissors
of a hairdresser hard at
work on your new 'do

Life Is Good

· 788 ·

Trying to do toe touches
with your friends and laughing about
everyone's lack of flexibility

· 789 ·

The neighborhood
smoothie shop

· 790 ·

Perfectly worn and
frayed jean jackets

Life Is Good

· 791 ·

Handfuls of fresh bread
dipped in rich olive oil

· 792 ·

How pigeons bob
their heads

· 793 ·

Your little corner in the
bookstore (and how dare
anyone else ever sit there!)

Life Is Good

· 794 ·

A grandmother's recipe
for lasagna from scratch

· 795 ·

Majestic Clydesdale horses

· 796 ·

The smack, smack of
pinball flippers at work

· 797 ·

Crunchy, tart Nerds candy

· 798 ·

All of Elton John's sunglasses

· 799 ·

The perfect cherry that
comes in your cocktail

· 800 ·

The little baby in the
Mardi Gras King Cakes

Life Is Good

· 801 ·

The soft whirring
of ceiling fans over
a back porch

· 802 ·

Tigger's bouncy style

· 803 ·

The cool, round,
hard feel of a blue
marble in your palm

Life Is Good

· 804 ·

Big stacks of buttery, syrupy
IHOP pancakes, right when
you're craving them

· 805 ·

The relaxing tones of wind chimes
tinkling in the back yard

· 806 ·

Peanut butter crackers
sticking to the roof
of your mouth

Life Is Good

· 807 ·

Recipe books with lots
of pictures that help you along

· 808 ·

The way dandelion
seeds float across the yard
looking for a place to root

· 809 ·

The rich smell
inside a cedar chest,
closet, or armoire

· 810 ·

The clanking sound of the
chain that pulls a roller coaster
up its first hill, and that subtle jerk
when it first catches the car

· 811 ·

The harmony of yin and yang

· 812 ·

Cars with dogs hanging
their heads out the windows
to catch the breeze

Life Is Good

· 813 ·

Platypuses—they're just
perversely fascinating to study

· 814 ·

Old-fashioned black-and-white
family photographs of couples
and children standing in front
of vintage automobiles and
squinting in the sun

· 815 ·

Kellogg's corn flakes

• 816 •

The funny sound of canned whipped
cream being squirted on strawberry
shortcake or cherry Jell-O

• 817 •

The colorful neon signs sprinkled
through your favorite bar district

• 818 •

Receiving a knowing glance from
your spouse or significant other
in regards to an inside joke

• 819 •

How the chocolate and
marshmallows perfectly smoosh
together in an ideal s'more

• 820 •

Crunchy sugar cubes

• 821 •

The humming of an airplane's
engines during your flight

Life Is Good

· 822 ·

Yards full of yummy
pecans after the pecan trees
rain down their bounty

· 823 ·

The smooth, rich feeling
of applying lipstick

· 824 ·

Little bags of peanuts and
pretzels on airplanes

• 825 •

Indiana Jones's faithful hat

• 826 •

Lemon-scented cleaning
products that leave your house
smelling super-clean

• 827 •

The hard POP!
of a racquetball against
the wall in a court

Life Is Good

· 828 ·

The goopy feel of hair conditioner

· 829 ·

The safe feeling of being wrapped
in a worn but warm flannel shirt

· 830 ·

B. B. King's music and legacy

· 831 ·

Little girls in dainty
pink Easter dresses

Life Is Good

· 832 ·

The adrenaline rush
of a walk through a well-crafted
haunted house in October

· 833 ·

Disneyworld vacations
(Go ahead and wear those ears!)

· 834 ·

A steaming pile of
chili-and-cheese fries

Life Is Good

· 835 ·

The pleasant sound of the air
conditioner kicking on

· 836 ·

Thick lashes brushing
against your cheek for
a dainty butterfly kiss

· 837 ·

The subtly ridged lines
of corduroy pants

Life Is Good

· 838 ·

Train whistles sounding
in the distance

· 839 ·

The sheen of a photograph

· 840 ·

The explosion of mums' vibrant
oranges and reds in the fall garden

· 841 ·

Those colorful stacks of coupons
you take to the grocery store

Life Is Good

· 842 ·

The whirring and hovering
of a fat bumblebee at work in
your garden's fresh blooms

· 843 ·

A kiss behind the ear

· 844 ·

Koala bears

· 845 ·

The way horses flick their
tails as they graze in a field

Life Is Good

· 846 ·

The spritzing sound
of yard sprinklers flicking on
to hose down the grass

· 847 ·

Viewings of *Singing in the Rain*

· 848 ·

The funny souls who
cover their cars with
bumper stickers

Life Is Good

· 849 ·

The rapid-fire way professional
blackjack dealers whip the cards
across to players at casino tables

· 850 ·

The fleshy and slick feel
of a wriggly frog in hand

· 851 ·

Helicopter rides over
the Grand Canyon

Life Is Good

· 852 ·

The pensive and evocative
music streaming from the
violin strings of a master

· 853 ·

Rich, ornate stationery
made of thick paper stock

· 854 ·

Full-body Swedish massages
where every sore inch of you
is soothed into relaxation

Life Is Good

· 855 ·

The pattering sound
of raindrops on top of your
faithful umbrella

· 856 ·

Older ladies in stylish,
fancy hats

· 857 ·

Four-leaf clovers—no matter
how old you are you still
feel you've hit the lottery
when you discover one

Life Is Good

· 858 ·

Bob Marley's full musical repertoire

· 859 ·

Lopsided berets

· 860 ·

Slightly overcooked hot dogs
hot from the patio's grill in
summertime that are smothered
with relish and mustard

Life Is Good

· 861 ·

The awesome sound
of white water rumbling
and challenging you to
bring in the raft

· 862 ·

Folk festivals composed
of artisan and craft booths
and food vendors offering
funnel cakes, ice creams,
and roasted corn cobs

Life Is Good

· 863 ·

Walks along long piers when
it's breezy and the pelicans are
clamoring at the fishermen
for a taste of the day's catch

· 864 ·

The funny charm, pendant,
or other memento you
superstitiously hang on to for
luck, be it a rabbit's foot,
a St. Christopher's medal,
or a pretty rock

Life Is Good

· 865 ·

The smell of freshly
bathed puppies and dogs

· 866 ·

The gentle pumping
sound of the soap dispenser
at the kitchen sink

· 867 ·

Dogs that hold their leashes
in their mouths during walks

Life Is Good

· 868 ·

Squishing Play-Doh around
to create your own "Mr. Bill"

· 869 ·

The way little foals
leap and frolic at the
horse farms in spring

· 870 ·

The wonderful earthy smell
on your hands from mulching
the flower beds and trees

· 871 ·

The *ding!* as you complete a line on
an old-fashioned typewriter (though
one is hard to come by nowadays)

· 872 ·

Perfectly steamed green
beans that squeak against
your teeth as you chew

· 873 ·

The fun and rebellious
feeling of sitting bare-bottomed
on darn near anything

· 874 ·

Christmas cards that
arrive in hordes

· 875 ·

The power, might, and grit
displayed by petite gymnasts

· 876 ·

The powerful tones
of old-fashioned school and
church bells set in motion by
pulling long, frayed ropes

Life Is Good

· 877 ·

The instant cool-down to your
forehead provided by a glass or soda
can dripping with condensation

· 878 ·

Dedicated UFO enthusiasts who
keep vigilantly looking upward and
informing us of anything new

· 879 ·

The sound of a bartender
whipping up the perfect martini
in a stainless-steel shaker

Life Is Good

· 880 ·

The inscriptions from friends
and relatives in the older books
of your personal collection

· 881 ·

The movie *Say Anything*

· 882 ·

How great the dinner table
looks when you make the effort
to bring out the wedding china

Life Is Good

· 883 ·

Shadow-puppet theater
on bedroom walls

· 884 ·

Ken and Barbie's many
humorous incarnations

· 885 ·

The darkness and constant cool
temperature of a hidden cave

Life Is Good

· 886 ·

The bumpy feel of a scab

· 887 ·

The hum of cicadas
outside a cabin's windows

· 888 ·

Shiny pennies